Milet Publishing
Smallfields Cottage, Cox Green
Rudgwick, Horsham, West Sussex
RH12 3DE England
info@milet.com
www.milet.com
www.milet.co.uk

First English–German edition published by Milet Publishing in 2013

Copyright © Milet Publishing, 2013

ISBN 978 1 84059 777 6

Original Turkish text written by Erdem Seçmen
Translated to English by Alvin Parmar and adapted by Milet

Illustrated by Chris Dittopoulos
Designed by Christangelos Seferiadis

Printed and bound in Turkey by Ertem Matbaası

My Bilingual Book

Hearing
Das Hören

English–German

Our ears are like our radar

Unsere Ohren sind wie ein eigenes Radar,

for hearing sounds from far.

mit ihnen hören wir Geräusche – ob fern, ob nah.

Our ears delight in hearing shouts of glee.

Am liebsten hören wir Jubelschreie voll Glück,

I am happy for you, and you are happy for me.

du freust dich für mich und ich freu' mich zurück.

Do you hear that buzz? Oh no . . .

Kannst Du das Surren hören? Oh nein . . .

It's a mosquito!

Es ist eine Mücke!

The sweet voice of my mother

Die süße Stimme der Mama,

is a sound like no other.

ist ein Klang wie kein anderer.

Hearing is a very sensitive sense.

Das Hören ist ein sehr empfindlicher Sinn,

We hear sounds and also silence.

wir hören bei Geräuschen und bei Stille hin.

When there's too much noise,

In einem lauten Gewimmel,

it's hard to hear one voice.

hört man nur schwer eine Stimme.

I hear the sound of propellers, so I know

Höre ich das Brummen sich nähernder Propeller,

it's a traffic helicopter, flying low.

fliegt wieder der Verkehrshubschrauber tief und schneller.

If we could listen to music all day long,

Hörten wir Musik, den ganzen Tag lang,

we would learn the words to every song!

könnten wir alle Liedtexte auswendig dann!

Our ears are for hearing what's around us,

Mit den Ohren hören wir die Welt um uns herum,

and also for listening to what's inside us.

aber auch die Dinge ganz tief in uns drin.

Morning brings a happy noise,

Bei Tagesanbruch hört man den feinen Klang

the sound of birds chirping, singing their joys!

von zwitschernden Vögeln mit ihrer Lieder Gesang!